Sam's First Hike

Story by Diana Noonan
Illustrations by Alejandra Barajas

Sam's First Hike

Text: Diana Noonan
Publishers: Tania Mazzeo and Eliza Webb
Series consultant: Amanda Sutera
  Hands on Heads Consulting
Editor: Gemma Smith
Project editor: Annabel Smith
Designer: Jess Kelly
Project designer: Danielle Maccarone
Illustrations: Alejandra Barajas
Production controller: Renee Tome

NovaStar

Text © 2024 Cengage Learning Australia Pty Limited
Illustrations © 2024 Cengage Learning Australia Pty Limited

ISBN 978 0 17 033385 6

Cengage Learning Australia
Level 5, 80 Dorcas Street
Southbank VIC 3006 Australia
Phone: 1300 790 853
Email: aust.nelsonprimary@cengage.com

For learning solutions, visit **cengage.com.au**

Printed in China by 1010 Printing International Ltd
1 2 3 4 5 6 7 28 27 26 25 24

*Nelson acknowledges the Traditional Owners and Custodians
of the lands of all First Nations Peoples. We pay respect
to Elders past and present, and extend that respect to
all First Nations Peoples today.*

Contents

Chapter 1

No Fun!

It was Friday night. Sam had been planning to spend the weekend at the bike park with his friends. But his mum wanted to take him on his first hike.

"Let's head for the mountains tomorrow!" said Mum. "We'll take my tent and camp for the night beside the track."

Mum loved hiking, and Sam sensed how much she wanted him to enjoy it, too. So he agreed to go.

The next morning, the sun was shining brightly. Sam and Mum drove to the start of the track.

"This is going to be fun!" said Mum, as they set off on the hike.

But Sam wasn't so sure.

Before long, Sam's backpack felt heavy and his feet hurt. "I need a break," he told Mum.

"Let's stop and have something to eat," said Mum, smiling. "We have plenty of time to get to our camp."

Mum took an apple out of her backpack. But just as she was about to pass it to Sam, a colourful bird flew down from the trees and tried to take it.

"Go away, you greedy bird!" shouted Sam. "That's *my* apple!"

Mum and Sam hiked all morning.
When they were almost at their camp,
they met another hiker. She was putting
up her tent beside the track. Several birds
were singing in the trees above.

"Hello! Are you staying here tonight?"
asked Mum.

"I sure am," replied the hiker. "It's such
a great place to listen to the birds."

Mum and Sam walked on, but Sam stopped suddenly when he saw some rough steps up ahead. There were at least twenty of them.

"They look dangerous," he said, with a shudder.

"They're very safe," said Mum, as Sam scrambled up the steps after her.

Chapter 2

Trouble at Camp

At the top of the steps, Sam and Mum reached their campsite. Sam was hot and tired.

"You have a rest," said Mum, as she took the billy can out of her backpack.
"I'm going to get some water. There's a little pond just around the next corner."

Sam sat down, but a few moments later,
he heard Mum yelling.

Sam rushed in the direction of the yelling.
He saw Mum by the edge of the pond.
She was all wet and muddy.

"I slipped and fell in the water,"
Mum groaned. "I've hurt my foot.
I can't walk."

"We can call for help on your phone," said Sam.

But Mum shook her head. "The phone got wet when I fell in. It won't work."

"I've got an idea," said Sam. "I'll go and find the hiker we met. I'll ask her to call for help."

"She's only ten minutes away," said Mum. "But are you sure you will be okay walking on your own?"

Although Sam was worried about the track and the big steps, he stayed calm. "I'll be okay," he said, bravely.

"If the hiker is not there, promise me you'll come straight back?" called Mum, as Sam took off.

"I promise," Sam called back.

Chapter 3

Alone on the Track

As Sam dashed along the track,
a colourful bird appeared ahead of him.
It looked just like the bird that had tried
to take his apple.

Sam looked at the bird as it flew
in front of him, beneath the trees.
"Thanks!" he called to it. "I could do with
a friend right now!"

At the steps, Sam went down carefully.
He kept his balance, and then walked
on quickly.

Soon, Sam spotted the hiker.

"Help! My mum is in trouble!" he called
out to her, as the colourful bird flew off.

The hiker's name was Lindy. She called the police right away.

"They said they'll send a rescue helicopter," she told Sam. "Now, let's go and check on your mum."

Chapter 4

Helicopter Rescue

Half an hour later, Mum was being lifted into the helicopter.

"You must have been afraid going down the track alone," she said to Sam, as he was buckled into his seat.

"I wasn't too scared," Sam told her. "And I wasn't alone. I had that colourful bird with me!"

"Well, I think you're very brave," Mum said. "And a very good hiker."

"Thanks," said Sam. "When your foot is better, maybe we could go hiking again?"

Mum looked at him in amazement.

"At first, I thought hiking wasn't much fun," said Sam, with a grin. "But now, I like it – especially the birds you get to meet!"